# Lewis's Daughter

by

Treva Carol Walker Barnes Tindol Dawson

Copyright © 2015 by Treva Carol Walker Barnes Tindol Dawson
All Rights Reserved

Published by Shadow Ridge Graphics through
CreateSpace.com

# *Lewis's Daughter*

My grandparents had nineteen grandchildren (I was number eighteen) and thirty-nine great-grandchildren. I came along after most of the great-grandchildren had already been born. Needless to say my grandparents had a problem remembering my name, so ... I grew up being called "Lewis's Daughter."

This is my story.

# Daddy

Lewis Carroll Walker was the oldest son of Pink and Letty Walker. He was born on March 19th, 1904 in Oran, Palo Pinto County in Texas, and died June 1st, 1989 in Seymour, Baylor County, Texas. He is buried in Oran Cemetery in Palo Pinto County.

He and his three sisters and his brother lived on a farm near Oran where Daddy attended school in a three-story building. The only things remaining in Oran today are a few houses and the cemetery. When the Walker family lived there, the little town had a railroad station and several hotels and all the benefits of a thriving little community.

When Daddy was about twelve he got into big trouble with his father. He had an aunt who owned a grocery store that he passed by every day on his way home from school. She would give him a stick of licorice whenever he stopped by ... so he began being later and later in getting home. Grandpa scolded him for getting home late, but he didn't stop going by his Aunt's store. One day, Grandpa went to his school and waited for him to get out. In Daddy's words, "He kicked my butt every third step all the way home." Their farm was several miles away out in the country, and Daddy wasn't late getting home after that.

On the 1920 census Daddy was fifteen years old, living at home with Grandpa and Grandma in Graford and working at a cotton gin. On the 1930 census he was twenty-six and still living at home in Graford, working on the family farm.

*Daddy was working at this filling station in 1932, where Mama and Daddy met.*

*Mama said she filled up her car as often as she could!*

*Before Mama and Daddy married in 1934*

In 1939 they had a child, who they named Treva Carol. Mom said there was an [Native American] Indian girl named Treva working at the Baker Hotel in Mineral Wells when she and Aunt 'Cille worked there. I have met very few in my lifetime with that name.

On the 1940 census, Grandpa and Grandma were living at 1401 SW 4th Avenue in Mineral Wells, Texas.

*Grandma (Letty) and Grandpa (Pink) Walker – about 1941*

*(I'm seen in the background, bringing in the milk – being very helpful)*

The little house is still there. I was able to go inside of it a couple of years ago when they were doing some renovations and no one was living there. It was just as I remembered, only much smaller. The old chinaberry tree that every grandchild and great-grandchild must have climbed was still in the front yard. I also remember climbing in that tree. This is where we went for Christmas and Thanksgiving every year.

*One of the cousins in the chinaberry tree*

*Lewis and Iva Walker with little Treva in 1941*

8

*Daddy and his family*

*Jerry Pink (called JP), Dorothy Idell Sears (the youngest),
Daddy (the oldest),
Millie Odetta Wilder, and Pearl Tipton Cooper
with Daddy's mother Letty May (Tipton),
and his father, Pinkney (Pink) Plunkett Walker*

# Mama

Iva May Lauderdale James Walker was born June 15, 1905 in Opal, Wise County, Texas and died in Bowie, Montague County, Texas on May 9, 1999. She is buried in Oran Cemetery in Palo Pinto County next to Daddy.

Iva May was the oldest of five children. Her siblings were Ida Lucille (Aunt 'Cille), Benjamin Franklin (Uncle Jack), James Melvin (Uncle Jimmy), and Mary Virginia (Aunt Jenny).

*Momma and her family*

*Iva May, Virginia, Lucille, Mama Dale, Jimmy, and Jack*

Mother's family was living in Salesville, Palo Pinto County, when she married the boy next door, Clark James. She was fifteen. Mama quit school in the ninth grade and moved into the house next door with her husband and her in-laws, Mr. and Mrs. James. She loved her mother-in- law, but her father-in-law was "as mean as a junk yard dog." (He died sitting in the outdoor privy and Mom said it served him right). Mom said that Clark James had just as bad a temper as his father.

They had a son, Billy Jack James, born on July 1, 1922. He died on September 7, 1967 in Mineral Wells.

A daughter, Dorothy Lavon James, was born on August 2, 1927. She died on December 2, 1928 of diphtheria. She was so small that her cradle was a drawer in Mama's dresser. Her death was a devastating blow to Mama. She and Clark divorced in 1929. Divorces were uncommon in those times.

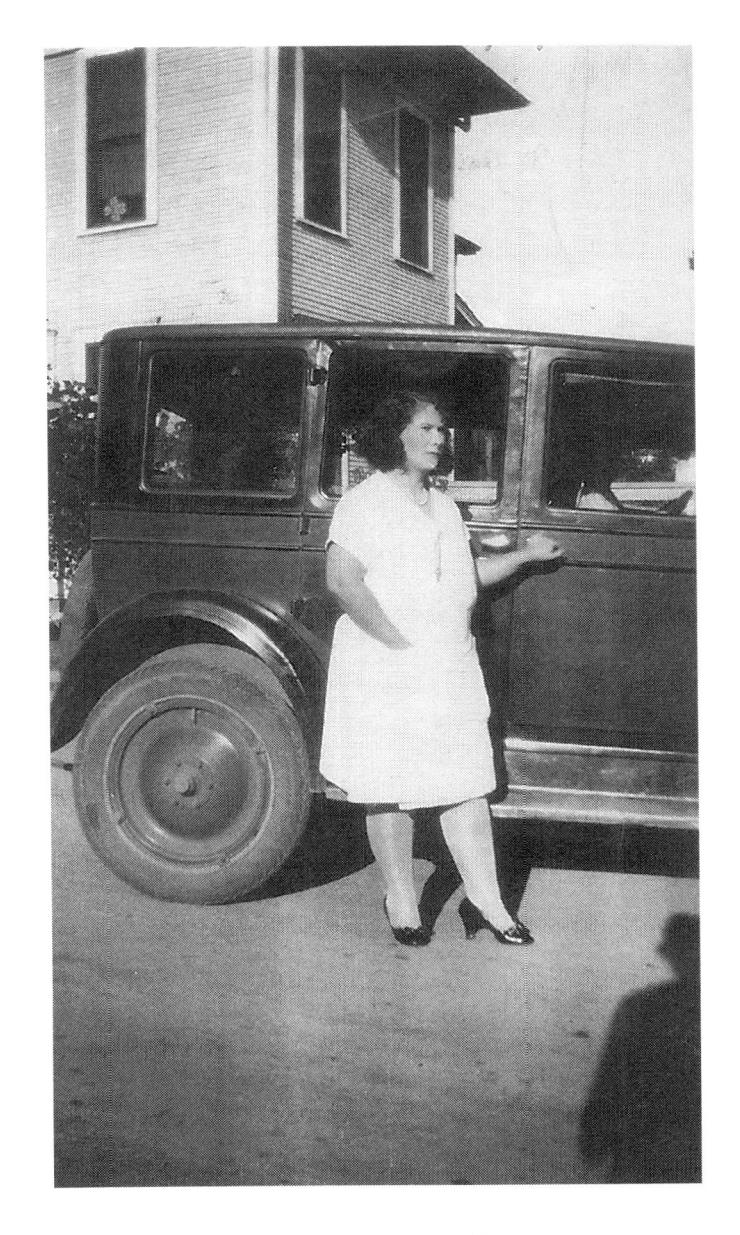

*Mama in Wichita Falls, 1925*

*On the back of the photo she wrote:
"This is our car - 400 Special Ha, Ha"*

Mama and her sister (Aunt 'Cille) lived together in Mineral Wells, and they worked at the Baker Hotel as waitresses. Both of them threatened me within an inch of my life if I ever became a waitress. I never was a waitress.

Mama always called her oldest child "My son, Bill" so that is what I called him ... SonBill. He lived with Mom and Aunt 'Cille in Mineral Wells after the divorce.

## Mama and Daddy

Iva and Bill were married on November 10, 1934 in Graford, Texas. Mom said that on their wedding day they went to a friend's house and helped them render a hog.

For over fifty years, Daddy called Mama "Wife" which was a very enduring term when he said it. I also remember him calling her "Ivey." She called him "Bill" as did everyone else. I can't remember Daddy being very outwardly affectionate to Mama or myself, but there was never a doubt in my mind that Mama and I were the most important people in his life.

Mama and Daddy had a happy marriage. I never remember them arguing or even raising their voices to each other. Mama would stay a few days with me when I had babies or when I was sick, but they spent very few nights apart from each other. Until Daddy died, Mama had never spent a night alone.

After we moved to Seymour when I was in the second grade, Daddy worked for the city in the Street Department for the next fifty years. When he retired he was the Superintendent of the Street Department and received a gold watch. He was so proud of that watch.

Daddy would come home for lunch every day and park the "grader" beside the house. Mom would have lunch ready. They ate at the old green and chrome Formica table in the kitchen by the window. At the end of every meal Daddy would say, "Just need a little something sweet, Wife." Mama always had a little something sweet ready to serve. Her peach cobblers and homemade hot rolls were two of her specialties.

Besides being a good cook and an immaculate housekeeper (she always made me make my bed and then she would remake it), she was an excellent seamstress. She made all of my clothes. She would see something in a store window or something some other little girl was wearing and make her own patterns. I had very few "store bought" clothes until I left home. She also made clothes for her grandchildren.

Mama worked at Buck's Fashion Shop for many years. After Mama retired, she stayed busy with alterations. She was so good that her customers would not let her quit.

Bea and Elzo Roe were longtime friends of Mama and Daddy. They met when they were working on the railroad together. They moved to Seymour when Elzo retired and they remained good friends for many years. Mama's best friend was Elsie Duggan (she was the daughter of Uncle Looney who was Grandma's brother).

Mama was in charge of organizing food for funerals and most other church activities that involved a kitchen. She was also a "Pink Lady" at the hospital for many years. She always loved to help others ... she was a servant.

On many occasions, I would find Daddy sitting on the front porch talking to someone about a problem. He was a wise man, and he had little use for foolishness. He was slow to anger like Grandpa, but not quite as patient. I think the word that best describes Daddy, and the reason so many sought his counsel, was because he was a man of *integrity*. He was introverted and shied away from anything that brought attention to him. He would serve communion at church, but only to the back rows, and he also helped count the money. After he retired he mowed lawns (for free) for the widows in our congregation. I remember him saying, "gotta go mow the old ladies' lawns" ... they were all younger than Daddy. He was a servant as well.

My parents didn't make much money. I had everything I needed but not everything I wanted ... except for one Christmas when I was in Junior High. The fad then was to have a leather jacket with long fringe on the sleeves and around the bottom. "All the girls have one," was my plea. I got the jacket and I was delighted, but that Christmas there was only that one gift under the tree.

I also remember when I was about ten that I got a Christmas present from Daddy that he had picked out himself. That was the most special gift I ever received. It was a black purse.

After Daddy died, Mama was living in Seymour by herself and doing well until she had a car wreck. She said she was coming home from church singing and not paying attention. She ran into a deep ditch and demolished her car. It was a wonder that she wasn't hurt more than she was. When she came home from the hospital, she came to Bowie to live with me.

## Treva Carol

My journey began on January 31, 1939 in the front room of Grandma and Grandpa Walker's house. An early birth certificate says Mineral Wells but a later one says Polk (have no idea where that came from ... we never lived in Polk). I've heard Mother tell the story of my birth a hundred times. The roads were icy, and Mom couldn't get to the hospital. Dr. Patterson (Doctor Pat) signed my birth certificate, but family lore has it that I came into this world before he could get there. This was the beginning of many years of having an icy birthday.

According to the 1940 census, we were living in Stephenville. I was nine months old. Billy Jack (he was Walker on the census) was sixteen. As soon as he turned seventeen, he joined the United States Cavalry and took back his birth name, James. He was stationed in Brownsville in South Texas and he was in the Cavalry Band. He played the Euphonium (smaller than a tuba and larger that a baritone). He was a good musician. I remember him telling me about riding a horse from Brownsville to El Paso along the Rio Grande as part of his boot camp. Sadly, he had the same temperament as his father.

*SonBill and his wife, Ruth*

We would visit SonBill whenever we went to Mineral Wells to visit Grandpa and Grandma. He was married to a wonderful woman, Ruth Drake, and they had three children. Barbara Ann, the oldest, was only four years younger than I. Dorothy Lavone and Billy Jack Jr. were the two younger children. Both Billy Jack and Dorothy are deceased. Barbara lives in Granbury.

Barbara and I were very close growing up. She would come every summer after we settled in Seymour and spend several weeks with us. I tried to make Barbara call me "Aunt Treva," but she never would. One summer I decided to give Barbara a haircut. Mama was really upset with me ... poor Barbara, she looked dreadful when she went back home.

## Early Childhood

When we were living in Stevensville, Mother took me with her to the grocery store. She stood me on the counter as she checked out her groceries. A contest was underway to advertise a new kind of rug that had been displayed on the street in front of the store. There were lots of little children all dressed up in their finest, standing on the counter for the judges to see. With me clinging to my bottle, and the toes cut out of my shoes ... I won the contest.

*May 31, 1940 – 16 months old – standing on the rug display*

I had my picture taken standing on the Pabco Rug, still clutching my bottle, with the "Walker frown" on my face. Mother wrote on the back of the picture that it was published in a magazine, but I've never been able to find the magazine.

I didn't stay with a baby sitter very often, but when we lived in Weatherford my babysitter was a young girl whose name was Mary Martin (the original Peter Pan).

Daddy got a job, repairing track along the railroad. He was a bulldozer operator. Daddy wouldn't be separated from us, so wherever he went ... we went too. Moving was a major influence on my life. I didn't realize until several years ago when I was at a ladies' meeting, how different my early childhood had been from theirs. We were talking about our first memories. I had no early memories of pets, or friends, or of special occasions. I never went on an Easter egg hunt, went trick or treating, or had a birthday party for the first six years of my life.

*My first birthday party when I was six ... Post, Texas*

Sonya and Donna Cooper lived in Mineral Wells, and they were my second cousins close to my age. When we became teenagers, they would sometimes find a date for me when we came to Grandpa and Grandma's. That was exciting. I dated very little in High School. I have lost touch with both of them now.

Sonya lives in Brownwood. Donna married into a family named Carlock that owned the funeral home in Mineral Wells. I also had a cousin (Rhonda Hankins) that went to Abilene Christian College at the same time I did. She lives in Lawton, Oklahoma.

# Early Memories

I have only a few memories before first grade. My earliest memory was of an event in Mineral Wells. A locomotive ran off the track. Mama and Daddy and I went to see the wreck, as did most of the townspeople. The locomotive was lying on its side with smoke billowing from all around it ... and it hissed. It looked like a giant monster to me and I went into hysterics. I still remember the fear and the panic, and I'm still afraid of being close to a train's engine to this day.

I remember when we lived in Bluff Dale, up on a hill. There was an open-air tabernacle right behind our apartment and they had very noisy meetings. I played with cutout paper dolls from the Sears and Roebuck Catalogue. To stay out of Mama's way, I played under the kitchen table. I remember listening to "Let's Pretend" and "Buster Brown" on Saturday mornings, and walking down the hill and across a highway with a teenage girl who lived nearby. We could get a coke float for ten cents at the drug store.

When we lived in Glenn Rose, I built a playhouse under a big tree next to a fenced-in lot whose sole occupant was a cow. I had a little ruby ring that was my birthday present and I was so proud of it. I was leaning over the fence talking to the cow, when I dropped my ring and I saw the cow eat it. I was so upset. Mom said I could go check the cow patties to find my ring ... but I couldn't bring myself to do that.

Another time when we lived in Glenn Rose (which was a health resort because of the sulfur water), I became very sick. Mom took me back to Mineral Wells to see Doctor Pat. I had typhoid fever and was one of the first ever treated with the new sulfa drug.

We lived in the little town of Woodson (the two blocks of downtown had wooden sidewalks ... and still does)! We lived in a house that had a picket fence around the back yard. Snakes had been killed in the neighborhood so Mom told me to watch out for snakes. I was walking on the railing of the picket fence in the back yard so the snakes couldn't get me, when I felt something touch the back of my leg. I thought it was a snake. I went running and screaming at the top of my lungs around the back yard. I thought the snake was nipping at my legs. Mom and the lady who owned the house had a hard time catching me. The sashes of my dress had come untied and they were hitting the backs of my legs with every step I took ... scared me to death.

We lived in "the other side of the house" with a sweet lady in Throckmorton. She was an old maid and she was the organist for the Baptist Church. I loved to listen to her practice. She told me the story of being engaged and her intended disappearing just before the wedding. She showed me the old yellowed wedding dress she had kept all those years in her trunk.

This is also where I climbed a tree and got on the roof of the house and couldn't get back down. Mom had the whole town looking for me and finally discovered me on the roof. The fire department had to get me down. Boy, was I in trouble.

# Education

It was in Post that we discovered that I couldn't see very well. I got my first pair of glasses in Snyder, Texas ... tiny, tiny little things (I still have them). We lived in an old hospital that had been converted into apartments (It's a museum today). One day, I gathered a bucket of horny toads (that's what we called them back then) and gave each apartment a little gift. Having to play by myself lead to a number of inventive things that got me into trouble.

We had already moved a number of times after I started first grade, and it was the last six weeks of school when we moved to Granbury. On the first day I went to school, the teacher told the class that everyone could go to the library at the back of the room. All the other children crowded around the library shelves and I couldn't get to the books, so I scooted across the round library table in the corner to get to the books. The teacher jerked me up by the hair of my head and reamed me out in front of everyone. I was dreadfully shy and I had never been treated that way in my life, so at the first chance presented to me, I escaped and ran home as fast as I could.

Mother took me back a couple of times and I would come back home as soon as the teacher's back was turned. Mom switched me all the way back several times ... there wasn't any way I was going near that teacher ever again. Momma was so worried that she took me to the doctor. He said there wasn't anything wrong with me, and that I just needed to change teachers. I was transferred to the other teacher's room and I was fine until school was out. The principal told Mom that he was going to pass me to second grade, but that I would never do well in school until I could go to a school longer than four to six weeks at a time. That was when Daddy decided to find a permanent home for us.

## The Move to Seymour

Daddy became the maintainer operator for the City of Seymour and I started second grade the next year. I never moved again until I graduated from high school. The little girl who sat behind me in second grade (Roxie Burkett) helped me to learn to read, but it took awhile for me to catch up.

We lived with Mrs. Johnson the first summer that we moved to Seymour. We lived in the other side of her house. She was a sweet lady and she would let me brush her long hair. It was here that I met my very first friend. She was a little black girl that lived right behind us in a little house not much bigger than a garage. We played together all that summer. It wasn't far to the icehouse from our house and Mom let me go with Leatha May to get ice for her mother. We took her little red wagon and got the ice, but we lollygagged along the way too much. Her mother whipped her and told her she could never play with me again. I was crushed. She said Leatha May didn't need any little white girl for a friend. I never saw Leatha May again after we moved from Mrs. Johnson's house. Back then, the black children would go to the black school until they were in Junior High and then they were bussed to another town to go to school.

We moved into Mrs. Fancher's house the next summer and we lived in the other side of her house. It was one of the coldest winters ever in Seymour. We had huge icicles hanging from the roof, bigger than I could put my arms around. There was a small pond in the park where I saw people ice skating for the first time. We walked to town to see a movie, "The High and the Mighty." That was the first and only time we ever went to a movie together. Mom would let me go on Saturday sometimes because the eye doctor recommended it. I had a lazy eye. I would watch a movie with a patch over my better eye and then watch it again without the patch so I could see what was going on.

That spring I found a little calico kitten in the trashcan in the alley. Mrs. Fancher wouldn't allow pets, so I kept her in an old hen house out back. She was my first pet ... "Kittyquay Kissyputten."

In fourth grade we moved into the first house that we had ever lived in by ourselves. It was a little two-bedroom stucco house on Tackett Street ... and I took my kitty with me.

Kittyquay Kissyputten had kittens and I kept one, which I named "Thomas J. Kissyputten." He was a big white cat that I had for a long time. He slept in a doghouse just outside the back door.

It was in fourth or fifth grade that I had my first migraine. We didn't know what it was back then. I would get sick at school and throw up and have an awful headache. It was thought to be a problem with my eyes so I would get a new prescription for my glasses. That never helped. All I could do was stay in a dark room until the headache went away. They have been a plague all of my life.

Letty Walker, my grandmother, also had those headaches. The headaches and arthritis were the reasons they moved from New Mexico back to Mineral Wells. She said the mineral water helped her. (it does have some lithium in the water). Daddy didn't have them, but they were passed on to me and I'm so sorry that I have passed them on to my children and even to some of my grandchildren.

I took piano lessons in fourth through sixth grade. I only practiced when I was supposed to wash the dishes after dinner. Mom wouldn't make me do the dishes if I practiced. I have always regretted not learning to play well.

*Age 12, May 26, 1951*

*My first recital*

In elementary school, I was a liability instead of an asset at recess ... accept when we played softball. I was small enough to crawl underneath the old army barracks, which were our classrooms. They weren't very far off the ground and I was the only one small enough to crawl underneath them and get the ball. No matter that there were spider webs and all other kinds of unknown creepy-crawly things lurking under there ... I had a purpose.

It was one of those times when I wasn't part of a team, when I decided to go into my classroom during recess. No one was allowed in the room during recess. To this day, I have a vivid memory of walking into that silent classroom. The sun was shining through the windows around the top of the room making streaks of light all the way to the floor, and you could see all kind of things floating in the rays. I also remember the smell of the red stuff that was used to clean the wooden floors.

Laying on each of our desks was our lunch money waiting to be collected after recess (I think it was thirty cents). I scooped up all of the lunch money and put it into my school bag, which was hanging at the back of the room, and went back outside. It was quite a surprise when everyone returned and all the lunch money was gone. The teacher said, "No one is leaving this room until that money is found!" She had us put everything on top of our desks and she checked each of our desks and our clothing. When she didn't find anything, she had each of us come up to her desk one at a time and she interrogated us. When she asked me, "Did you take that money?" of course, I said no. Because I was so quiet and shy, she never thought that I could have been the culprit. And, she never checked the stuff on the hangers at the back of the room. I've always wondered about that. Maybe it was God's way of teaching a small girl a big lesson (It's better to get caught than to get away with it). She and the principal finally decided it must have been someone from another class who took the money.

On the way home I stopped at a gas station and bought a Pepsi Cola and a Baby Ruth. Then I went to a vacant lot close to my house and hid the rest of the money under a bush. It's probably still there to this day. I couldn't drink my Pepsi or eat my candy bar. For years I would wake in the middle of the night and remember: "I'm a thief." I finally confessed when a bunch of girls at Abilene Christian were discussing early memories. I've told that story many times since then. When I was a counselor and the subject of stealing came up, it was a good object lesson. I think I've told it to all of the grandchildren as well. It was my dear grandson, Madison, who wanted to go back to Seymour and see if the money was still under the bush where I hid it.

When I was in sixth grade I was the Halloween Queen ... not because of popularity, but because I raised the most money in the Halloween contest. The Halloween King was Ruben Crenshaw. He lived at the lake and he was my first boyfriend. After high school he became a well-known rodeo clown, and was later killed by a bull.

Things began to change for the better when I reached Junior High. I finally had enough friends to have another birthday party and I started playing the French Horn in the Band.

(from left to right)
Top Row: Betty, Carol Jean; Second Row: Ann, Bobbie Jo, Roxie; Bottom Row: Judy, Trellis, Lou

I carried my French Horn, which was almost as big as I was, home (across town) every day. I became First Chair French Horn in high school and was selected to played in the regional band. I was offered a band scholarship from several colleges when I graduated.

# Friends

I met Ann Studer (Gee) at church. She became my best friend. We were best friends all through junior high and high school. I remember spending the night with her in the country. She had no heat in her room and she had to get up early the help her mom cook breakfast for their large family. We were baptized at the same time in sixth grade and we were roommates at Abilene Christian. She was an inch shorter than I was.

Carolene Hash (Stoveall) has also been a friend for the last fifty years. I was in her wedding and she was my Maid of Honor. Her family had a cabin at Lake Kemp and it was a treat to go with her when the first day of May was celebrated in Seymour. Everyone called it "Fish Day." All the businesses would close down and everyone would go to the lake. Her dad would catch fish and her mother would fry them. I have never tasted anything any better in my life. Mother said I couldn't go out in their boat, but that was all right, because Carolene and I liked to sun bathe on the boat dock. Her father owned the Buick dealership and it was fun when we would go with him to pick up new cars. We each got to drive a brand new Buick back to Seymour.

Judy Church (Starr) was a friend who I still see whenever I go back to Seymour. She and her husband, John, moved back to Seymour after they retired. She is the only one left in our hometown who was a friend in high school.  Judy is an expert at carving eggshells.  She made a beautiful carving for Sam and I as a wedding gift.

I can't remember the last time I saw Roxie (the little girl that helped me learn to read), but when she found out I had authored a book, she bought more of them than I've ever sold to any one person.  She was so proud of me.

We moved across town to a neat little house on Cedar Street when I was in ninth grade.  It was just a block from the high school.  Mom was working at Buck's Fashion Shop so I got to eat lunch with my friends.  I never once ate in the school cafeteria.  We ate at the Rock Inn Cafe on the Lubbock Highway.  It was only two blocks from school and it's still there to this day.  I had French fries and a Dr. Pepper every day and we listened to Lefty Ferizzell on the jukebox.  Whenever I get puny and nothing sounds good to eat, I can always eat French fries (not the crisp fast-food kind ... the good old-fashioned greasy kind).

It was the best of times in which to grow up.  Seymour was a small town, a farming community where there were lots of good people ... and gas was cheap back then.  On Sunday afternoons one of us would get the family car and we would make the drag from the Dairy Queen to the Courthouse and back again.  There were no drugs, no gangs, and no violence (that I knew of).  All of the boys had guns in their pickups and it wasn't a problem.  It was a way of life.  The boys would occasionally be very naughty and go "cow tipping" at night. If they did anything worse than that, I didn't know about it and I also didn't know what "cow tipping" was ... still don't. I had a record player and my pastime was listening to Perry Como and Patty Page. It was a time of innocence.

When I was a junior in High School I entered a writing contest. The subject was, "Why I Want to Go to the United Nations." I won fourth place in the Texas competition. Along with winners from New Mexico, Oklahoma and Arkansas, and some teens from an orphanage, we embarked on a three-week bus trip to New York City with stops at historical places along the way. Boy howdy, did this small town girl's eyes get opened! I had never been any farther from home than Oklahoma City. I almost didn't get to go on this trip. Mama wasn't going to let her little chick out of the nest. I had to threaten to move to Aunt 'Cille's house and Aunt 'Cille told Mom she was going to come get me if she didn't let me go. From that time on, I knew that outside of Seymour ... there was a big, big world.

When I was a senior, the high school counselor told me that I wasn't college material. I knew I wasn't nearly as smart as many of my classmates. Looking back, the valedictorian of our class earned a Doctorate degree. She and I have more degrees than any other kids in our class.

*Graduation*

## The Move to Abilene

I graduated in 1957. I quit my job as cashier at the Texas Theater, and Ann Studer and I were off to Abilene Christian College (ACC) together that summer. Mama and Daddy borrowed money for my tuition and I worked on the switchboard in McKinsie Dorm (twenty five cents an hour) and I had a band scholarship.

My freshman year at ACC my English teacher told me I was spelling on a third-grade level and that she didn't see how I could make it through college. I had done all right in summer school and I had dodged having to take entrance exams, which I probably couldn't have passed. I had a "C" average when I graduated, with a degree in Education. After student teaching, I decided that teaching wasn't for me. I went back to school and received a Masters of Education Degree in Counseling (I had a "B" average). I received certification as a Licensed Professional Counselor on the 16th of August, 1983. I have also published two historical novels, co-authored a history book and a book of poetry ... not bad for someone who can't spell or punctuate. The work ethics that I learned from my mom and dad enabled me to overcome obstacles.

I was in the band that first summer at ACC when I met Peggy and Jerry Drennan. Peggy has been my best friend since 1957 and will be until one of has to say goodbye.

I also met Carroll Moffett, Jerry's best friend. We dated that summer and most of the next year. He was a good guy, even if he did go to Hardin Simmons, a rival university in Abilene. He played French Horn in the Cowboy Band. I hadn't had but a few dates in high school and I wanted to "test the water." I broke his heart and I've always regretted that.

Most students on a band scholarship had their own instrument. I didn't have one, so Carroll helped me search the pawnshops for a "horn." He and I played in the Abilene Symphony Orchestra and that is where I learned to love classical music. I also played in the Abilene Community Band for eight years after I moved to Avenue F. When I moved to Bowie, I put up my horn, but I still have it. It's an antique, now.

During my junior year, a young man who had just gotten out of the Army came to ACC. He was a very good French horn player and quickly became the First Chair "horn" in the band. I was impressed with this outgoing, confidant and good-looking young man. What he saw in me is still a mystery.

*Glenn and I*
*He was meeting Mom and Dad for the first time*

Band tours in the summer (Peggy was always my roommate because married couples couldn't stay together), along with the Band's musical production for the student body are some of my favorite memories. Almost all of my friends in college were members of "The Big Purple."

I was in the Pandora's Social Club my sophomore year. We built a huge Purple People Eater for a homecoming display.

My roommate, Ann, got married after our freshman year. Ruane Lassater (Renninger) was my second roommate, and we have remained in contact with each other over the years. I lived in McKensie Dorm both my freshman and sophomore years.

# Marriage and Children

Glenn Barnes, Jr. and I were married on August 23, 1959. It was a big wedding at the Seymour Church of Christ with a reception in our preacher's home.

Carolene was my Maid of Honor along with Ruane and a couple of other friends from ACC. The music was recordings from ACC's Acapella Chorus.

Our first home in Abilene was a two-story garage apartment directly across the street from the College Church of Christ. Neither of us had graduated so we were still attending ACC and our parents were still helping us. When we found that we were expecting our first child, we bought our first home. It was a little house on Questa

Street near Dyess Air force Base. We both finished college the summer of 1961.

Kelly Ruane was born on May 13, 1961. I was so big carrying Kelly that people felt sorry for me and that would make me cry. Kelly was a big baby ... eight pounds and thirteen ounces.

Kelly was a happy child and she was always smiling. She walked before she ever had a tooth in her head (I know it's hard to believe, but then she was almost ten months old when she was born). She was mobile in a walker at five months. She cut her hand on a can lid in the trash and when I took her to the doctor, he didn't believe me. They would have strung me up for child abuse these days. Kelly was taking a few steps on her own at seven months. When she became mobile, she took off and hasn't stopped since. She didn't crawl, which caused her to be dyslexic.

Kelly has always been "a doer and a people pleaser."

*Kelly Ruane Barnes*

When a house became available next door to the Drennans, we moved to Buccaneer Street. We were living there when Whitney Carol was born on November 29, 1962.

*Whitney Carol Barnes*

Whitney turned over so much that she wore the bottom part of her hair off and all that was left was what Aunty called "hair that hung up." I was beginning to think she didn't have a smidgen of human kindness in her until she found an old half-dead cat and cared for it until it died. She has been a caregiver ever since.

When Whitney was in kindergarten, someone was pouring bleach on the floor in the kindergarten bathroom. When the culprit was finally caught, it turned out to be Whitney. She has always been a little mischievous, and she was always able to talk her sister into things that would get Kelly in trouble and she would come out smelling like a rose.

*July 1965*

The girls were almost the same heights, and I dressed them alike so most people thought they were twins. They were inseparable ... and still are, which has always pleased me very much.

When Jerry was offered a position at ACC, the Drennans moved to the "Hill". Peggy became the music teacher at Taylor Elementary and they built an A-frame house on Rountree. It wasn't long before we followed suit. We built next door ... the same floor plan. Kendall Goldman came along on August 1st, 1967 and that completed our family.

*Kendall Goldman Barnes*

Kendall was a quiet child, but he didn't need to talk ... his sisters did it for him. Their job was to get him ready for church on Sunday morning. They had all kinds of trouble getting his shoes on him. I can still remember them complaining, "Mama, he's curling his toes up again!" He had this cute little innocent smile, but he knew exactly what he was doing ... and still does when you see that smile. I couldn't have asked for better children. They were and still are my most treasured blessings.

I finished my Masters in Guidance and Counseling in 1968 and went to work for Abilene Christian Schools (called the Campus School) as an All Levels Counselor. I had to have three years' experience in the classroom to be certified. About the same time, Nancy Thompson completed her degree in Administration and she also needed teaching experience, so ... we split teaching the seventh grade for three years. She taught the hard stuff - math, science, and language arts - and I took Texas History (which I loved), reading and PE (I had never had a PE class in High School and only a badminton class in college).

Nancy taught half a day and I taught the other half. I was the All Levels Counselor half time, and she was the elementary Principal half time. We both became full time after we completed our requirements.

I was a counselor at Abilene Christian Schools for seventeen years. At one point, all of the administration had to teach a class. I taught Texas History for three years and loved it. All three children graduated from ACHS.

A couple at church, Roy and Bonnie Shake, had a bunch of children of their own, but they began keeping foster children for Christian Homes of Abilene. That is how we became involved with foster care. Our first foster baby was Little Ann. We brought her home from the hospital and kept her for five months. When she was placed with adoptive parents, it was like losing a child of our own. We grieved until we took a second baby, Bobby. He stayed with us for four months and we went through the same grieving process all over again. That is when we began taking older children.

Daisy was about five months old when she came to us from an abusive home. She became the mascot for the softball team on which the girls played and Glenn coached. They made it to the playoffs and the team didn't think they could win unless Daisy was there. That was another hard loss when she was adopted.

There were others that stayed shorter amounts of time until Jimmy came to live with us.

We weren't sure of Jimmy's age because he didn't know how old he was. He and his little sister were left with a babysitter when his mother disappeared. We put him in first grade and he stayed with us for three years. The girls had to learn how to defend themselves. Even back then, he would lie when the truth was staring him in the face. He came back several times while he was in other foster homes. The last time was after he got out of prison. After lying on the couch smoking all day for several weeks, I took him out of town and dumped him on the highway in the freezing rain. That was one of the hardest things I have ever done. I used to get letters from him and they always started with "Dear Mom." He always thought of me as his mom. He died in prison.

Life changing events began to occur when Glenn decided he wanted to farm. He bought land in west Texas and became a cotton farmer. The children and I stayed in Abilene. I was the only source of income. He would come home every weekend and then every other weekend and soon he was spending extended amounts of time out west. One day Kelly became ill and I couldn't get in touch with Glenn where he was supposed to be. That was when I learned that he was living with a woman who had three children. When he came home he wanted a divorce. It was a very difficult time for me, and the children. Dub Orr (an elder at Willis) convinced Glenn to return to us, but irreparable harm had been done to the marriage.

The Drennans were off on a missionary trip when a nice two-story house on Avenue F became available. We moved while the Drennans were gone ... I don't think Peggy has ever forgiven me for that. There was a gate between our two back yards and we ate together several times a week and our kids grew up together. Their two children, Cohn and Hollis, were our children's close friends and playmates.

It was nice for each of the children to have their own bedroom in the new house. Kelly was neat and Whitney was not (just to drive Kelly crazy, I think). Having their own rooms solved a lot of problems. Our lives were full of basketball, football, track and other school activities until they finished high school.

Kelly was small, but unusually skillful when it came to sports. She could dribble the basketball backwards as well as she could forward. We called it "doodle-bugging." Whitney was always the leader on the teams. They were both cheerleaders and involved in all of the school activities. Kendall played football, basketball, and ran track. He didn't get his growth until he got out of high school, so he was always the smallest on his teams. I still remember seeing him go flying through the air every time he got hit in a football game.

Whenever Kelly's class needed anything done, Kelly was the "go to" person ... and still is. Whitney was a leader. She was president of her class for all four years of high school. Kendall was quieter and more reserved, but everybody loved Kendall.

It was about that time that the bottom fell out again. Glenn found another girlfriend. That was it for me. I took Kendall and our clothes and moved into a little house on East North 16th Street. It wasn't long before Glenn asked for a divorce so he could remarry. It was an uncontested divorce.

Glenn's parents were Pop and Bess. Pop was a wonderful man. He was happy, always laughing and kind. Bess was self-centered, sometimes downright mean, and she thought she was better than everyone else. She always had to have the best of everything (matching leather gloves, purse and shoes). She was a Dotson, and she came from money and influence, and she never let anyone forget it. She raised her son to feel the same way. He could never do any wrong in her eyes, and I could never live up to her expectations. I wasn't from the right social status (I didn't know which fork to use). Glenn's sister, Virginia, was a lot like their father. She was delightful and all of us loved her. Bess had a sister "Aunty" who was an "old maid schoolteacher," and we all also loved Aunty.

After the divorce Kendall and I moved back to Avenue F. The girls were going to ACC. Kelly got married, and then Whitney got married. They found two fine young men (Jimmy and Jim) who became my sons-in-law.

Kendall and I got on with our lives, and things returned to normal ... until a new school was built. They were top-heavy with administration, but I think having a divorced counselor wasn't what they wanted either, so my counselor's position was eliminated.

## The Move to Bowie

After seventeen years at the Christian School, I had to find a new job. I was visiting with Mom and Dad and decided to go to the Wichita Falls Educational Service Center. They knew of openings for several counselor positions in the area, so I began interviewing. In 1986, Kendall and I moved to Bowie where I became the Junior High counselor for the next seventeen years.

This was a life-changing event for me. I realized that I could support Kendall and myself and I could make decisions on my own. After living for twenty-three years under Glenn's contentiousness and controlling behavior, I was finally able to find myself and again recover the person I used to be.

Kendall had just graduated from high school and the move was harder for him than it was for me. Even though I had to leave the best friends that I had ever had, Kendall also had to leave his friends. He tried going to Midwestern and several different Junior colleges, but he finally gave up and went to work. Harvey helped him get into an apprentice program with the Sheet Metal Association.

Thanks to a loan from Dub Orr, I was able to buy the old Baptist parsonage where we were living. When my house on Avenue F in Abilene caught fire, Peggy called me from her school and told me it was burning. After collecting insurance on the house, I was able to pay off my note to Dub.

My children and my wonderful sons-in-law helped Kendall and I repaint the 1940s house and get it spruced up. I loved that old house. It was big and roomy and it had a cross on the chimney. After we sold it back to the Baptists, they gave it to the city for a controlled burn. That broke my heart and I haven't forgiven the Baptists yet.

Daddy became ill with pancreatic cancer and died on June 1st, 1989. Kelly, Whitney, and I took turns going to Seymour to help Mom take care of Daddy. It was a labor of love and we were glad we were able to help Mom. It also gave us a chance to spend some time with Daddy during his last days. Daddy was my anchor and I still miss him.

Mom, who had never spent a night in her life by herself, was doing well living by herself after Daddy's death until she had a car accident. It was then that she moved to Bowie to live with me.

The time that Mom and I had together after Daddy's death was a blessing. I was always very close to both of my parents and I was the most important person in their lives (until the grandchildren began to come along). It was hard for Mom to sell most of her "stuff" that she had collected over the years and move, but she was glad to be with me and I was thankful she was there. She was always my best friend, as well as my mother.

Life for me began to change as well. I met a rawboned old fellow who stole my heart. He loved me and he loved Mom. William Harvey Tindol and I eloped to Ardmore, Oklahoma on April 17, 1992. We were married by the Justice of the Peace, which was about as different from my first wedding as you could get. Harvey wore his boots and jeans and a baseball cap. I don't even remember what I wore.

We didn't have a honeymoon. We came back home because I had to go back to school. I was keeping Lady, Kendall's dog, for him and she had a "thing" about someone being on the other side of a door. When we got home, I stuck my head out of the door to say hello to Lady and she jumped up and bit me on the nose. My nose was a terrible looking thing. It swelled up and turned bright red. I had to return to school looking that way. The faculty had a field day with that.

Mom was still pretty active and still cooked lunch for us every day. I remember one time when Harvey got home for lunch before I did and Mom was standing on the kitchen cabinet trying to reach something on a top shelf ... it liked to have scared him to death. Mom cooked lunch until she began to forget to turn off the burners, but she could still make the best peach cobblers and homemade hot rolls that anyone has ever tasted. All of us still treasure her recipes.

Mom and I went to church together, but Harvey didn't go. He was from a "holy roller" background and didn't have much use for church. Mom always looked so cute all dressed up and everybody at church loved her.

As Momma got older she began to leave the house and she couldn't find her way back. I got several calls at school from the police asking if I knew an Iva Walker. That is when we began having someone stay with her during the day. All of her sitters thought she was the sweetest little lady they had ever known. When she got to the point where she didn't know where she was, we put her in a nursing home. I regret that until this day. They just didn't take good enough care of her. She had to get up early and take a shower. While she was with me she could sleep until she woke up and take a bath in a heated bathroom. She was like a little "hot house flower." She got cold easily and I kept her warm. Mom had to be hospitalized several times while she was in the nursing home, but she made so many miraculous recoveries after receiving blood transfusions that we began to advise everyone who was sick to "get a transfusion." It's still one of our remedies for illness.

I don't want to forget the grandchildren: Kelly and Jimmy's children are Chase, and Corbin. Whitney and Jim's children are Grayson, Madison, and Tiffany.

(from left to right)
Madison, Chase, Tiffany, Corbin, Grayson

There are lots of great-grandchildren as well. When the Lord said, "go forth and multiply," my grandchildren evidently thought He was speaking directly to them. The four boys have graduated with degrees and advanced degrees and Tiffany will soon have her degree. I am very proud of all of them.

Kendall married a beautiful girl, but the marriage didn't work out. He has been gun-shy ever since and has remained single. His sisters and I were very glad when he left Nevada and returned to Texas. All three children have stayed close to each other, for which I am so very thankful. The girls have been at the science department for Fort Worth Christian School for over thirty years and Kendall has continued to work for the Sheet Metal Association.

Harvey and I moved the year after Mama died. We found this lovely old two-story Victorian built in 1891. We removed all of the old layers of wallpaper, and the gold and green shag carpet, and the pink tin cabinets in the kitchen, and did our best to restore it. We have been on the Christmas Tour of Homes several times and people still ring the doorbell and ask if they can look inside the house. I think this is the oldest house in Bowie. We put a three-tiered fountain in the yard where one used to be when the house was young.

*Harvey, the house, and the fountain*

    Harvey was a good businessman. He bought land and built a used car lot, complete with a mechanic, Harvey Throneberry. We have always called him "Big Harvey." He became our partner in Double H Auto Sales and Wrecker Service. We also began to buy small houses and refurbish them. Harvey fixed the structural problems and I made them livable. We had a number of heated discussions about the houses, but we worked well together. He never had a problem with speaking his mind and I was determined to never let anyone run over me again. We always worked it out.

Harvey had two grown children, Ginger and Gayla. Ginger has two girls, Arron and Emilie, and Gayla has an older son, Spencer, and twins, Mason and Madeleine. I have always loved Harvey's girls. Gayla and Brian live in Bowie. Ginger and Neil live in Colleyville. They and their children are still part of my family.

One of the happiest days of my life was when Harvey became a Christian. He couldn't carry a tune in a bucket, and he didn't know much Bible, but from then on we were at church whenever "the doors opened." Jerry came to Bowie and baptized him. Jerry also performed all three of the children's weddings and Mother's funeral.

Harvey was as strong as an ox until he had kidney failure. He always liked to get up and go whenever he wanted and he never sat still for very long. He handled being tied down by dialysis with grace and dignity for three years. I was so proud of him. He said "that's my job now." He died on April 26, 2008. He was cremated with one-third of his ashes buried next to his first wife in Bowie, one-third to his children, and one-third in a jar in my china cabinet to be buried with me.

I've always been an avid reader. I use to disappear and the kids would find me hidden in the laundry room where I could read. It never entered my mind that someday I would become a writer. Here is another mysterious way in which God has worked in my life.

    I became the One-Act Play Director when I was at ACHS, and I also helped Peggy write original skits for her choir productions. When I moved to Bowie I continued directing plays. Some of the one-act play scripts were so awful that I decided I could write a play just as good as the ones I was using. The first play I wrote was also awful. The second one was better, and I won first in the UIL competition with the third play. The writing bug had bitten. In Ancestry Magazine there was a place where one could send in an original short story. The first one I submitted was about Mama's china cup tradition. It was accepted and they actually paid me for it. I wrote another and it was accepted and then they decided to eliminate the writer's page. In the meantime, I had begun to get into genealogy and build our family tree. From that came the inspiration for the first book about Sam and Milley Walker (Daddy's grandparents) "Flowers for Milley" followed by "Forks in the Road." The last book, still being written is "Feathers of Green," which will be the third book in the trilogy.

    Judy Berry edited the first book and Gale Cochran-Smith edited the second book. They could punctuate and spell really well. Together, Gale and I have written a history book, "Memories Along the Chisholm Trail" and a book of poetry, "Reflections in Two Voices." We are working on a sequel to the Memories book. Gale is one of the best friends I've ever had. She and Sam have their work cut out for them trying to take care of me.

Growing up alone and having to entertain myself has given me the gift of imagination, which is essential for a writer. With help from spell check, and really good proofreaders, I've been able to do what I love to do the most ... to write. I had no idea how my books would be accepted, but the feedback and encouragement from my readers have "fueled the fire," so to speak.

Many times I've been asked where I obtained the artwork on the covers of the books. I am always proud to say that my grandson, Corbin, is the creator of the artwork. Gale is also a talented graphic designer and artist, and arranged Corbin's artwork on the covers of the books.

On August 23, 2009, I was on the church bus going to a church event with some friends when I received a strange call. It was Glenn reminding me that it was fifty years ago that were married. I had been working on forgiving him since we divorced, but I had never really succeeded. It is a wonderful feeling to be able to put all of the old bad memories in the past and finally fully forgive. We have been friends since then and I am truly thankful that I no longer have to live with the dark cloud of un-forgive-ness.

I am disappointed that Glenn has not been closer to his children or accepted them into his family, although Kendall has been accepted more than his daughters have been. There have been times when I would have liked to call Glenn to ask him a question or just to check on him to see how he was, but there would have been consequences for any contact with an ex-wife.

I was the counselor at ACHS for seventeen years, the counselor at Bowie Junior High School for seventeen years, and then I retired. I wasn't quite ready to completely retire so I opened a private counseling practice in my home. It was called Roundtable Family Practice. We met around Mom's old round oak table. I really enjoyed private practice more than school counseling because my clients came because they wanted to come instead of being sent to the Counselor's office. After ten years in private practice, I did finally retire.

I loved Harvey with all my heart, and I took care of him to the best of my ability while he was on dialysis. I grieved his loss until one day I realized ... I had to go on without him. That day, under the Wisteria Vine in the back yard, I played for God to send me someone to love again ... and God answered my prayer. He sent me Sam.

I became acquainted with Sam Dawson online. He was a member of the church and he wrote books on Biblical subjects. He was a retired Physicist, a retired preacher in the Church of Christ, and retired from

Microsoft. We communicated online for close to a year and we came to know each other reasonably well ... kind of like a couple in the past writing to each other to get acquainted. We became good friends.

We met when Sam was on his way to a family reunion. He decided he might as well stop by to see "that lady he had been emailing" since he was coming through Bowie. It didn't take long for us to decide that we wanted to spend the rest of our lives together. This time the wedding was here in my old house. It was a lovely wedding. Kendall gave me away, and the girls were my bridesmaids.

The years that Sam and I have had together have been a blessing. We love being together and we especially enjoy traveling together. My children are very grateful that he is a good driver and that he doesn't mind "Driving Miss Daisy." He is kind, considerate, and loves to laugh. He is also the most dedicated and knowledgeable Bible scholar I've ever known and I am still in awe of his brainpower. We treasure each day we have together, knowing that one day one of us will have to go on without the other.

Sam finds himself needing to take care of me more and more. I can't remember things that are important to remember and it seems to be getting worse quickly. Mostly it is short-term memory, but who knows when the long-term will begin to go. That is why I decided to get some of my memories in writing. There is hardly a day that goes by that I don't wish that I had asked Mom and Dad and my grandparents more questions. I hope this writing will help answer questions that my family and friends may have as time goes by. Recalling these remembrances has been an enjoyable trip down memory lane.

Whatever I have been able to accomplish in my life is because of the loving home my parents provided, the work ethics they demonstrated, and the sacrifices they made for me. No one could have had better parents and I couldn't have had better children and grandchildren.

It is my prayer that we will all be together again in the hereafter.

## Some Favorite Memories

The trip to New York City when I was in high school with the stops along the way was a life-changing event.

Glenn and I and the children and Mom went to Disneyland in California. Kendall stood in the front seat the entire way and Mama and the girls were in the back seat. Mama would make sandwiches for us while we traveled. When we went to Disneyland and we lost Whitney. We found her at the "Lost Parents" booth, calmly eating an ice cream cone. She wasn't the least bit upset, but we were beside ourselves.

Kelly, Whitney, Kendall, Kerry (Whitney and Kelly's best friend) and I went on a vacation in Acapulco, Mexico (we were all skinny then).

Madison bought tickets to a Ranger game (with his own money). We had good seats, the game lasted twelve innings, there were fireworks after the game, and I had my first beer.

Tiffany came down to spend a few days with me when she was learning to drive. We explored almost every dirt road in Montague County (sometimes pretty close to the ditch). She was also in one of the plays that I wrote and directed for Chicken and Bread Days. She stole the show.

Peggy and I went to Scotland and England. We went on a bus tour of the Highlands and then rented a car to see the Borders. We stayed in Lauderdale, Scotland and visited Thirlestane Castle (where my ancestors, the Maitlands of Lauderdale, had lived).

Peggy, our friend Carol, and I traveled somewhere together many summer until Peggy had to go on dialysis. Since Peggy has been on dialysis, Peggy, Jerry, Sam, and I meet halfway between Abilene and Bowie as often as we can and have lunch together.

My friend Janet (my principal's wife and fellow teacher) and I had an antiques store in downtown Bowie. We didn't sell a lot but we enjoyed going to estate sales and auctions. That is where I obtained most of my vintage furniture. I remember when Janet and I and our spouses parked outside an old home in Bowie and spent the night in the car so we could be first in line when the doors opened.

My friend Carolyn and I went on a Caribbean Cruise and I won a thousand dollars in a slots tournament. I didn't have a clue about what I was doing. It was announced over the ship's intercom that "A little lady from Texas" won the tournament. It was my claim to fame.

Gale Cochran-Smith and I did a lot of traveling together to collect information and take pictures for the Memories Book. That was very enjoyable and we developed a special bond with each other.

Kelly, Whitney and Kendall came up together to Bowie and spent the night. We had such a good time together. We played games at the kitchen table that evening and we had our favorite "creamed eggs" for breakfast the next morning. I have always loved being with my children.

The first trip Sam and I took together was to see his little hometown of Cactus. It was the most pathetic little burg I've ever seen. It's a good thing he moved to Dumas to finish school and then on to Amarillo to go to Junior College. He went to Texas Tech, where he graduated with degrees in math and physics. We have taken a vacation every year since we've been married. The first trip was to the northwest. We went across Canada to Seattle, where Sam had spent a number of years as a physicist for Boeing, and where he began twenty-two years of preaching.

We have also gone to Savannah and down the coast to St. Augustine, and on to New Orleans. On our trip this year we saw Mount Rainier on the way to Vancouver, where we took a cruise ship to Alaska. On our way back home we stopped in San Francisco. Sam had a surprise for me that he had kept a BIG secret. It turned out to be the best surprise of my life.

We went to Spinnaker Restaurant in Sausalito, where we had a view of San Francisco Bay. Then we drove into San Francisco to see an off-Broadway production of "The Phantom of the Opera" in the beautifully restored Orpheum Theatre on Market Street. It was the first performance of the twenty-fifth season, and it was a magnificent production.

We plan to take other (shorter) trips for as long as we are able to travel.

This place has a special memory for all of us ... Mom and Dad's house in Seymour ...

... and last but not least, the silver tinsel Christmas tree.

*Treva Carol Walker Barnes Tindol Dawson*

# OUR GENEALOGY THROUGH THE GRANDPARENTS

## *The Walkers*

***** <u>**Edward Walker (my great, great, great, grandfather)**</u> was born at Isle of Wight, Virginia in 1745. He married his first wife, Nancy Larned, in 1776 at the High Hill Baptist Church in Louden County, Virginia. The children from this marriage were: Benjamin 1778; John Bird 1780; Mary 1781; and Nancy 1785. Nancy Larned Walker died in 1785 (most likely in childbirth) leaving four children with their father. The oldest was only seven years old.

Our lineage is through Edward's second wife, *"The Widow Carroll."* I think her name was Nancy Carroll, but that is not confirmed. They married in North Carolina about 1786 and had the following children:
Garrett 1787, Rockingham County, North Carolina; Louise 1789; William 1780; Sara 1795; and Samuel 1798.

**\*** <u>**Samuel Alexander Walker (my great, great, grandfather)**</u> was born on October 30, 1798 in North Carolina and died June 16, 1865 in Moniteau County, Missouri.

Samuel served as an Orderly Sergeant under Nathaniel Green's command at the Battle of Cowpens in the Revolutionary War. He was of English Decent.

Samuel Alexander married Agness Bradford born September 6, 1793 in Granville, North Carolina. They were married in 1817. Her father, Booker Bird Bradford, was also born in Virginia, of English decent and served in the Revolutionary War (there is a book written about the Bradfords).

While they were in Smith County, Tennessee, Samuel served as a deacon at the Bush Creek Primitive Baptist Church in Carthage, Tennessee. He and Agness, along with his older brother Bird, moved to Cole County, Missouri (which later became Moniteau County) in 1836. They both received a letter of dismissal from the church. Agness' father was also a member of that church (The little church is still there). Other names on the church's rolls show up later in the Walker family (Agee, Hooker, Barnett).

Samuel Alexander and Agness had nine children. Byrd Bates, Anna (Burk), Elizabeth (who died in her first year), Nancy (Etter), Francis (Agee), Sarah (Wilson, who was the submitter the first DAR paper), Samuel Carroll, Thomas Tuggle and William Madison.

An article about William Madison Walker appeared in the *History of Saline County, Missouri, Historical Company, St. Louis 1881:*  William Madison was the county tax collector for Saline County, Missouri for three terms.  In the article he says that when he was three years old, he and his family moved to Missouri where he was raised on a farm in Moniteau County. He was married to May Isabel Garrett.  They had nine children with one dying in infancy.  They moved to Moniteau County in 1836 where they spent the rest of their lives.

The part that was interesting in this article was its assessment of William Madison's character. "Industry, economy, perseverance, and a genial disposition will readily account for the steady increase of his estate and of his influence in the county," and  "His integrity is above suspicion and the people can find no fault with him as an official."

(Integrity is a word that has also been used to describe the character of both Pink Walker and Louis Walker).

* **_Samuel Carroll (my great grandfather)_** was born in Highpoint, Moniteau County, Missouri on May 5, 1828. He died February 5, 1893 in Millsap, Parker County, Texas. He married *Milley H. Matthews* who was also born in Moniteau County, Missouri on August 2, 1831.  She died in Jack County, Texas on June 22, 1880.

Sam and Milley moved to Lone Oak, Hunt County, Texas, from Missouri - along with his brother, Bird, and their thirteen children. Sam and Milley's children were William Thomas (Tom), John Dudley, Nancy Ellen (Ellie), and Samuel Madison (Matt). They were all born in Highpoint, Moniteau County, Missouri.

Whatever the reason that Bird and Sam found for moving, it must have been compelling enough to get the two brothers to leave their families in Missouri and travel by wagon with all their children and all their belongings to Lone Oak in Hunt County, Texas. Bird had thirteen children and Sam had four children at the time of their move.

Sam and Milley added two girls, Mary Morneau (Morey) and Agness Ann to the family and two more sons, Carroll and Edward H. (called Ned) while they were in Lone Oak. Sam was farming next door to the Hookers (from the little church in Tennessee) when the call went out for volunteers for the Confederacy. Sam mustered in on October 2, 1861 as a "saddler."

Bird was too old to join, but one of his sons, William Tuggle, also joined the Confederacy in Collin County. He was wounded and taken prisoner at the Battle of Stone River. He died and was buried in a mass grave. His body was later removed and buried again in the Confederate Circle of Heroes at the Evergreen Cemetery in Murfreesboro, Tennessee.

Bird decided to move again (he and all of his children) and of course, Sam moved with him. He and Milley and their eight children moved to Locust Bayou, in Calhoun County, Arkansas. On the 1800 census (I've never seen another like it), Sam and Milley were farming. They grew corn, had beehives, fruit trees, pigs, cattle, horses and nine children. They are all listed on the 1800 census, along with the newest member of the Walker family, baby Alexander, who was only three months old.

**_* Pinkney Plunkett Walker (my grandfather)_**. This is the story that Pink told, about how he came to have the name Pinkney Plunkett. His mother, Milley, was too ill to nurse when he was born so he stayed with the family who lived on the farm next door to them, who had a wet nurse (the Plunkett family is listed as next to the Walkers on the 1880 census). While he was with the Plunkett family, they called him Pinkney. That was the name that he came home with and the name that he had for the rest of his life. He may never have known that on the 1880 census, he had been given a family name ... Alexander.

Bird (who was a physician) lived the rest of his life in Arkansas, but Sam and their nine children moved back to North Texas, to Grayson County, where Ellie married Dick Dewberry and Tom married Eliza P. Cox (she was only fourteen). Tom and his family made every move his father and his family made until Samuel Carroll died in 1893.

Ellie (the oldest girl of Sam and Milley) told her grandson (who lives in Ardmore, Oklahoma) several stories about her mother and father (Sam and Milley) as she was growing up. He passed these stories on to me.

Ellie remembered seeing a scraggily bag of bones, walking up the road to their house in Grayson County, Texas. Her mother ran out of the house and started kissing the man in their front yard. It was Sam Walker coming home from the war. He had been a shoemaker in the army and had been discharged because of chronic dysentery.

She remembered when Sam and Milley and their children were traveling from Texas to Arkansas. They had an encounter with a cowboy along the trail who made a comment about Ellie. Her father took exception to the remark. He and the cowboy rode around a bend in the road to have a private discussion. After a while they heard a shot. Sam came back with the cowboy's horse in tow, but no sign of the cowboy. Sam tied the horse to the back of the wagon and they continued on their way. He never said what happened and they never asked.

Ellie said that she and the other children had to "dress" (take the cotton seed out of the cotton bolls) and fill their shoes before they could go to bed when they were young.

Ellie was quite an amazing woman. After her husband died (he had been a blacksmith), she was left with five children under the age of twelve. She stayed in Grayson County, kept her family together and provided for them.

When her children got older, they began to make trips to Indian Territory every chance they got, to visit their uncle Matt (he lived just across the Red River in Jimtown, Indian Territory). It wasn't long before she and her children relocated to Indian Territory to be closer to her brother.

She was sixty-six years old when her oldest son lost his wife. Ellie moved to his home and raised her five grandchildren who ranged in ages from eighteen months to fourteen years. (It was one of these children that told the stories to our Ardmore cousin, Wendell). Ellie died at the age of ninety-two and is buried in Shey Cemetery in Marshal County, Oklahoma.

Sam and Milley's oldest son, John, had already gone back to Missouri when their son, Samuel Madison, persuaded them to move again. The family joined Matt in Hillsboro, Texas.

Samuel Carroll didn't stay long in the Hill Country. He couldn't resist the call of the unsettled frontier in Jack County. Sam had promised Milley he would "put down roots," so he bought land about ten miles north of Jacksboro where he built a home for his family with his own hands. It was a cabin with a loft where the boys slept, two bedrooms downstairs, a kitchen and a common room. He also laid all the flat rock floors of the cabin. A well and a cellar were dug by hand, which completed the new home. Sam, with the help of his neighbor, Jim Stacy (he later became Morey's husband), established a herd of cattle and became a farmer and rancher. Tom and Eliza lived nearby. All was well until tragedy struck the family. Milley's health had been declining since the birth of Pink and she suddenly took a turn for the worse. She died on June 22, 1880 in Jack County when Pink (Grandpa) was ten years old.

It was difficult for the Walker family to adjust to Milley's death, so Sam decided to start over. He and his remaining children (Agness, Carroll, Ned and Pink), along with Tom and his family, Morey and her husband, Guadeloupe Victory Stacy (but they called him Jim) loaded their wagon, and moved to a little community called Ballew Springs in Parker County, Texas. Tom's family and Morey's families settled in Weatherford, not far from Sam. This is where Pink went to school for the first time. It was also where Sam later became acquainted with Elizabeth Frances Lamar Ironmonger, who lived in Millsap. She was a widow with three boys.

The Walker children didn't like Frances and called her "that Ironmonger woman." When she and Sam married, Sam and Agness moved into Frannie's big house in Millsap. They added four more children to the Walker family: Birdie (Kitty), 1885; Maggie Lee, 1887; Sara Frances (Sallie), 1889; and Stonewall Jackson, 1891. I met Stonewall Jackson (Jack) at a Walker reunion in Millsap.

Sam died on February 5, 1893. Frances lived many more years, dying on March 31, 1927.

FRANCES
wife of
S. C. WALKER
BORN
FEB 24 1850
DIED
MAR 31 1927
My mother slumbers here

Sam's three younger boys stayed on the farm and made their own way after Sam married Francis. Agness married Andy Hulen and moved to Palo Pinto County. It wasn't long before Agness had persuaded her younger brothers to move as well. Carroll was never much of a farmer so he became a wrangler for Agness and Andy. Pink and Ned tried their hand at farming. Pink was twenty-one when they rented a farm at Black Springs on Keechi Creek. The little town had only one store (the old rock store on Keechi Creek was where the town of Grayford was later built). On a farm nearby lived a prosperous farmer and rancher, Tobe Tipton and his wife Mattie, and this was where Pink met Letty Tipton. They married July 1, 1894 at Letty's home in Oran, Palo Pinto County, Texas. They farmed in the Oran area and at one time ran a dairy.

When Grandpa retired, he and Grandma moved to Mineral Wells to the little house on 4th Avenue, where they lived for the next thirty-nine years. Grandma died on May 11, 1959 in Mineral Wells, Texas.

Grandpa was ninety-three years old when he came to live with Mom and Dad. His dearest wish was to go back to Jack County and find his mother's grave, so Daddy and I took him to Jacksboro. We looked in the cemetery there, but we couldn't find Milley's grave. The courthouse in Jack County burned in 1880 and all the records were destroyed; there were no funeral home records. I've checked every cemetery in Jack County and found no information about where Milley is buried. The grave may have been so old that we couldn't find a marker or it may be somewhere else on private land or underneath Possum Kingdom Lake. It's still a mystery.

Pink Walker was ninety-four years old when he died on April 18, 1964 in Seymour. He is buried in Oran Cemetery next to Grandma. Carroll Walker and Agness Hulen are buried in Breckenridge, Texas.

## The Tiptons

* <u>**Letty May Tipton (my grandmother)**</u> was born on February 2, 1877 in Paint Rock, Jackson County, Alabama and grew up in Oran, Palo Pinto County, Texas. She was the great, granddaughter of Shadrick Tipton and Hanna Peters; the granddaughter of James Martin Tipton and Martha Penelope Brown; and the daughter of James Anderson "Tobe" Tipton and Susan Emmaline "Mattie" Bowers. The children of Tobe and Mattie were Ada Louisa, Dovie Pearl, (Dovie Pearl died when she was sixteen and is buried in Oran Cemetery) and four brothers. They were William (Will), James Luna, (Uncle Loony lived in Seymour with his wife, Elsie, who was Mama's best friend), Louis Moore (Grandma's twin), Letty May, and the youngest was Jeremiah (Jerry).

Pink and Letty had five children, Pearl Tipton (Cooper), Milley Odetta (Wilder) Lewis Carroll (daddy), Dorothy Idell (Sears), and Jerry Pink (called JP). One child (Nora Bell) died when she was less than two years old (there is a puzzling stone in the Oran Cemetery).

When Daddy was ten (1914), Grandpa and Grandma moved from Graford to the Sangre De Christos Mountains in New Mexico to be near Grandma's brother, Will. Daddy remembers the train ride from Mineral Wells to El Paso. It was his job to carry the dirty diaper bag. From there they traveled to the mountains in a wagon. One of his favorite memories was exchanging his sausage and biscuit lunch with a little Indian boy who he became friends with at school.

His Uncle Will was a tough character. One time Daddy wanted to go with his uncle across a mountain range. Daddy had to ride a mule and his uncle told him that if he couldn't keep up, he would go off and leave him ... which he did. Daddy had to find his way back home through the mountains by himself.

They left New Mexico and moved back to Texas because of Letty's health. She thought the mineral waters in Mineral Wells helped with her arthritis and her headaches. They lived in the Oran community until Grandpa retired. That is when they moved to Mineral Wells and lived there for thirty-nine years in the little house on 4th Avenue.

Grandma's rheumatoid arthritis had drawn her into a sitting position all of the years that I knew her. Her arms and her hands were also drawn into a fixed position. She was able to move around by herself in a cane bottom chair by shifting her weight and making it "walk." Grandpa had to take her to the bathroom, get her dressed and help her in and out of bed for many years. Their daughter, Pearl, took care of them after her husband died. When she died, Odetta took care of them after her husband died until Grandma died.

Mentally, Letty Walker, did not depend on anyone else. She was a "women's libber" before there was ever such a thing ... strong willed, determined and outspoken, but I never heard Grandma complain about her condition. Grandpa and Grandma were complete opposites in disposition, but it was a relationship that worked well. Grandma gave the orders and Grandpa carried them out.

Grandpa and Grandma were both Christians. Grandpa's father was a part-time Baptist preacher, and the Tiptons were members of the Church of Christ when they moved to Texas from Alabama. One of Grandpa's brothers, Edward (Ned) was one of the founders of the Church of Christ in Graford, Texas. There was a little one-room frame church building within walking distance from Grandpa's house in Mineral Wells. That is where he always attended church and I remember walking to church with him. At that time Mom and Dad didn't attend church.

Jerry Carroll (grandchild #19) came to visit the spring of 2015.  We hadn't seen each other in many years.  He and I were the only first cousins still living at that time.

## *The Lauderdales*

**\* _Elbert Lauderdale (my grandfather)_** was born in Lafette Mississippi on March 15th, 1879 and died in Wichita Falls on October 30, 1937, before I was born. His mother and father were James Robert Lauderdale and Susan Vaughn from Lafayette County, Mississippi. He and Mary Ferguson were married in Keeter, Texas in Wise County. (There is a sign on the highway outside of Decatur and a road to Keeter, but there is nothing there). Elbert was a barber and they moved a lot after he and my grandmother married. All of their children were born in Wise County, but in different towns except for one who was born in Floydada. (Mama remembers putting newspaper on the walls of their house to keep the cold from coming through the cracks when they lived in Floydada).

Mother and all her family inherited "the Lauderdale spread." They were all short, curly headed, and big in the rear like their father. Mom said that her father, Elbert Lauderdale, was a jolly person. He loved to play games and he loved baseball. He was the umpire for the Wichita Falls Sputters baseball team. I wish I could have known him. We could have enjoyed a baseball game together.

Mom, and her brothers and sisters all came from the same mold. All of them loved to laugh, play games and have a good time. Mama was the oldest child. She was four feet eleven inches tall. Her sister, Ida Lucille, was four feet ten inches tall. (Since I grew to be five feet tall, I always felt "tall"). Mama had two younger brothers: Benjamin Franklin (Uncle Jack) and James Melvin (Uncle Jimmy). Mary Virginia was the youngest child.

Aunt Lucille ('Cille) lived in Fort Worth at 2414 Circle Park Blvd. I can still see in my mind's eye every single room of her house.

At one time we lived in an apartment upstairs, but I don't know when it was. I remember looking out of the upstairs window. I loved to go visit Aunt 'Cille because I was her only niece and she loved me. Aunt 'Cille's only child was Marvin Earl Leuton, and Don Reeves was Aunt Virginia's only child. They were the only two cousins I had in the Lauderdale line. Marvin was much older and I, and I was never around him much. Don and I were closer in age, but our families didn't travel enough for us to build a close relationship.

Uncle Jimmy and Aunt Edna had a cabin at Lake Kemp near Seymour where the Lauderdales congregated. All the brothers and sisters (except Aunt Jenny) would get together every summer at the Lake.

Mom and I were always close to Uncle Jimmy and Aunt Edna. He worked for Panhandle Oil Co. in Wichita Falls, Texas from the time he was fourteen until he retired. They never had any children of their own so their inheritance was equally divided between thirty-eight nieces and nephews when they passed. I was the only one from Uncle Jimmy's side of the family to inherit (Aunt Edna had thirty-seven nieces and nephews). Cousin Don wasn't part of the inheritance because Uncle Jimmy didn't think he took care of his mother like he should. It was a nice inheritance for all the rest of us. We all received $30,000 each. They were very frugal. Uncle Jimmy's only extravagance was a new Cadillac every year. He didn't have anyone to show it to, so he would come to Seymour to visit every year until his death and we would take a ride in his new "Caddy."

I was able to trace the Lauderdale line back to Lauderdale, Scotland. They were known as Maitland of Lauderdale. When one of the children migrated to America, they dropped the Maitland name and the titles and took the name Lauderdale. On the wall of their castle is a painting of one of our Lauderdale ancestors. He has long, very curly red hair and he was a little chubby. Lots of our Lauderdales had curly red hair and were a little chubby. I visited the castle when Peggy and I were in Lauderdale, Scotland (Thirlestane Castle). The family invited me in when I told them of our connection. They showed me the dungeon and part of the castle that hadn't yet been restored. It was *very* rustic. The restored part was beautiful.

## *The Fergusons*

* <u>**Mary Jane Ferguson (my grandmother)**</u> was born in Leaton, Lawrence County, Alabama on September 15, 1885. She died in Seymour on the 26th of September, 1973. Her father was a doctor and Mary was his youngest child. She remembered traveling with him in their buggy when he made house calls. After her mother died, he remarried. At the age of twelve, she came to live with her sister, Tennie, in Wise County, Texas.

All of the Ferguson sisters were named for states: Tennie (Tennessee), Callie (California), Lucy (Louisiana), and Mary (Maryland). She met and married Elbert Lauderdale when she was seventeen.

I'm not sure what happened to Mama Dale, but all the years I knew her she a little "off-center." Mom thought it could have been because of a tragic accident that happened when her youngest son, Elbert, was playing along the railroad track near their home in Wichita Falls. He fell under a moving train and was killed. After that she was never the same.

After my grandfather died, she and Uncle Jimmy lived in a "flop house" in Wichita Falls. Uncle Jimmy had to go to work when he was fourteen (he was hired as an errand boy and worked for Panhandle Oil Co. for the next fifty years). I found them both listed on a 1940 census in Wichita Falls living in a house with about thirty other people. Uncle Jimmy stayed in Wichita Falls after he married Edna and that is when Mama Dale went to live with Aunt 'Cille for the next forty years.

Every summer, she would come to stay with us for a while to give Aunt 'Cille a break. I had to sleep with her and she would pinch me if I got close to her side of the bed. When she got older she came to live with Mom and Dad until her death.

She loved boys, but not girls (including me). She was mean to my girls, but she loved Kendall. Mom kept her as long as she could and then put her into a nursing home in Seymour, where she died several years later. I did not grieve her passing. She is laid to rest next to Aunt 'Cille in Oran Cemetery (I hope she doesn't pinch Aunt 'Cille).

Made in the USA
Columbia, SC
28 October 2022